Department of the Environment
Welsh Office

PPG7

CW01024091

PLANNING POLICY GUIDANCE:

THE COUNTRYSIDE AND THE RURAL ECONOMY

Contents

1. Policies for the countryside

Introduction

1.1 The White Paper *This Common Inheritance* sets out the Government's environmental strategy, including its policies for the countryside. These are based on sound stewardship of the heritage and on creating the conditions for a healthy and growing economy. The main aims are:

– to encourage economic activity in rural areas;

– to conserve and improve the landscape, and encourage opportunities for recreation;

– to conserve the diversity of our wildlife particularly by protecting and enhancing habitats.

1.2 Planning Policy Guidance notes set out the Government's policy on different issues, and how it relates to the preparation of development plans and the consideration of planning applications. This PPG provides policy guidance on the countryside and rural economy. It is for local authorities to determine the more specific policies that reflect the different types of countryside found in their areas. The first part sets out the Government's general policy approach, and how it should be reflected in land use planning policies. The second part provides more specific advice on different aspects of development in the countryside. That is followed by advice on planning policies in areas with special countryside designations. Special attention is drawn to the new policies for determining major planning applications in National Parks. The annexes provide detailed guidance on particular aspects, including the operation of the new controls over agricultural buildings which took effect on 2 January 1992.

Change in the countryside

1.3   The past thirty years have been a period of considerable change in the rural areas in England and Wales. Between the 1961 and 1971 Censuses the population of rural areas increased by 1.6 million, or nearly 18%, and between 1971 and 1981 another million, or nearly 10%, while the total population of England and Wales increased by only 5.7% and 0.5% in these two periods. Around 20% of the population live in the countryside, and those who work there contribute substantially to the Gross Domestic Product. Over most of the countryside, past trends of rural depopulation and high unemployment have been reversed and in many areas the rural economy is now thriving. But these overall statistics conceal a loss of younger population, and a change in the nature of employment, with declining opportunities in agriculture and traditional employment such as mining and quarrying. These structural changes will continue, and demand further action to diversify the rural economy.

1.4   The agricultural policies established after the war aimed to provide the nation with a reliable source of food at a reasonable price, and the farmer with a reasonable return. These policies were strengthened when the UK joined the European Community and resulted in increased output and food surpluses. Measures are now being taken to reduce the overall cost of support to the agricultural industry by increasing the role of market forces and by curtailing support and protection. This trend will continue. In addition, environmental objectives will be integrated further in agricultural support policies where practical and worthwhile. The result, for the first time this century, is that land is being taken out of production. This offers new opportunities and challenges. Landowners will need to look at a range of options for the economic use of their land, including expanded woodland planting, recreation and leisure enterprises and the restoration of damaged landscapes and habitats.

1.5   Agriculture will remain the major user of land in the countryside, but a decreasing one. It is not and will not be the main source of employment. Economic activity is growing apace in rural England. New types of commerce and industry, including those based on new technology, are locating in rural villages and small country towns. The quality of the environment in such areas clearly attracts such investment. Where problems remain, the Rural Development Commission works in England with local authorities, Rural

Community Councils and private investors to target assistance to priority areas. In Wales the Development Board for Rural Wales and the Welsh Development Agency perform a similar function.

Protecting the environment and encouraging the rural economy

1.6   The Government believes that it is important to sustain this process of diversification and to accommodate change, while continuing to conserve the full and varied countryside for the benefit and enjoyment of existing and new residents and visitors. In this way the rural economy can continue to prosper and expand, and make its own contribution to the quality of the environment. Maintaining a healthy rural economy is one of the best ways of protecting and improving the countryside because so much depends on the investment of people and other resources.

1.7   The Government promotes policies that help rural businesses to compete in the UK and internationally. These policies are being extended to the agricultural sector as it adapts to Common Agricultural Policy reform. Many farm businesses are developing closer links with the market and consumers. Nevertheless, some intervention in the market may be needed to ensure the proper protection and enhancement of the countryside. For this reason, financial support has been provided for practical conservation measures, and is backed by a framework of environmental regulation.

1.8   The Government seeks to integrate its policies for the countryside in a number of ways; for example, by including environmental objectives in agricultural and forestry policies and by encouraging high environmental standards in the implementation of rural development policies. The planning system is an important component of this policy.

1.9   Much activity in the countryside is outside the scope of planning control. But the planning system helps to integrate the development necessary to sustain the rural economy with protection of the countryside for the sake of its beauty, the diversity of its landscape, the wealth of its natural resources and its ecological, agricultural and recreational value.

Planning policies for the countryside

1.10   The guiding principle in the wider countryside is that development should benefit the rural economy and maintain or enhance the environment. The countryside can accommodate many forms of development without detriment, if the location and design of development is handled with sensitivity. New development in rural areas should be sensitively related to existing settlement patterns and to the historic, wildlife and landscape resources of the area. Building in the open countryside, away from existing settlements or from areas allocated for development in development plans, should be strictly controlled. In areas statutorily designated for their landscape, wildlife or historic qualities, policies give greater priority to restraint.

The role of development plans

1.11 Development plans are means by which development to sustain the rural economy can be accommodated while protecting the countryside. Development control decisions are required to accord with the development plan unless material considerations indicate otherwise (full advice is provided in PPGs 1 and 12).

1.12 The Government's *regional planning guidance* sets out regional policies of relevance to the preparation of development plans, and which are of a wider geographical basis than individual structure plans. The topics covered in that guidance will depend on the individual circumstances of each region, but will normally include the natural environment and rural development. In some regions, the existence of National Parks and Areas of Outstanding Natural Beauty are major strategic factors. (In Wales, the Welsh Office is producing for consultation a series of Strategic Planning Guidance in Wales reports, which may include advice on the countryside and the rural economy.)

1.13 *Structure Plans* (and Part 1 of Unitary Development Plans) should state the overall development strategy for the county/metropolitan district, indicating how the balance between conservation and development has been struck geographically. The general policies on new housing, conservation, the rural economy, major development, and tourism will all impinge on the countryside. *Local plans* (and Part 2 of UDPs) should set out more detailed policies and proposals as a clear guide to development control decisions. All plans are required to include policies in respect of the conservation of the natural beauty and amenity of the land.

Other planning guidance

1.14 Plans may be supplemented by guidance on such matters as the protection of landscape features or design guides for specified areas, but this does not have the same status as the development plans. Two other processes may inform the preparation of development plans – a systematic assessment of landscape character, and non-statutory rural strategies. The Countryside Commission has published advice on landscape assessment techniques (1). Some local authorities have prepared non-statutory countryside and rural strategies in cooperation with a wide range of rural interests. These can be a valuable means of coordinating the policies and priorities of organisations which affect the rural area concerned. Comprehensive strategies which integrate conservation with economic and social development can be a positive influence on development plans.

(1) Landscape Assessment: A Countryside Commission Approach (CCD 18,1987).

2. Development in the countryside

Introduction

2.1 The advice in this section applies to the countryside generally; special considerations which apply only in designated areas are covered in section 3. Most of our countryside carries no special designation. It is, nevertheless, valued by all who live and work there and by visitors. It is the Government's policy that the countryside should be safeguarded for its own sake and that non-renewable and natural resources should be afforded protection. Over the past 50 years, there have been unprecedented pressures on traditional landscapes and wildlife habitats. Some of these pressures have been due to development; others have come from changes in farming and forestry.

Land use changes and diversification

2.2 The success of the post-war policy of retaining agricultural land in full production can be seen by the decreasing amount of farmland transferred

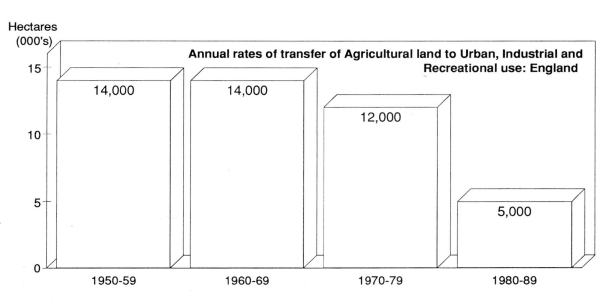

to urban uses, particularly in recent years, as shown in the diagram. Increases in the area and productivity of arable land, and reclamation of derelict land and other measures to stimulate urban renewal, have all contributed to these decreases. But it is the planning system that has been and will continue to be the principal means for regulating the rate at which land is transferred from agriculture, forestry and other rural uses, to urban, commercial and industrial use.

2.3 The increasing efficiency of agricultural producers and changes in agricultural policy mean that retaining as much land as possible in agricultural use no longer has the same priority. The priority now is to promote diversification of the rural economy so as to provide wide and varied employment opportunities for rural people, including those formerly employed in agriculture and related sectors.

Development plans and development control

2.4 When preparing their development plans and deciding applications for planning permission, local planning authorities should take account of any special designation (see the following chapter) and then weigh the following factors:

– the need to encourage rural enterprise;

– the need to protect landscape, wildlife habitats and historic features;

– the quality and versatility of land for use in agriculture, forestry and other rural enterprises (paragraph 2.6 below explains the special protection which applies to the best and most versatile agricultural land);

– the need to protect other non-renewable resources.

In assessing these factors, local planning authorities should bear in mind that once agricultural land is developed, even for "soft" uses such as golf courses, return to best quality agricultural use is seldom praticable; once any land is built on, the restoration of semi-natural and natural habitats and landscape features is rarely possible and usually expensive.

Protecting the best agricultural land

2.5 Annex A explains the agricultural land quality classification system. In preparing development plans and considering planning applications, authorities should take account of the quality of any agricultural land that would be lost through development proposals. Land of moderate or poor quality (grades 3b, 4 and 5) is the least significant in terms of the national agricultural interest. In making the assessment recommended in paragraph 2.4 above, little weight need normally be given to the loss of such land, except in areas such as hills and uplands where particular agricultural practices themselves contribute to the quality of the environment, or to the rural economy in some special way.

2.6 About one third of agricultural land in England and Wales is of grades 1, 2 and 3a. This is the best and most versatile land, and is a national resource for the future. In making the assessment recommended in paragraph 2.4, considerable weight should be given to protecting such land against development, because of its special importance. Within these grades, where there is a choice between sites of different classifications, development should be directed towards land of the lowest possible classification. Because of the national interest in protecting the best and most versatile agricultural land, the local planning authority are required to consult the Ministry of Agriculture, Fisheries and Food (in Wales, the Welsh Office) about any development that does not accord with the development plan and which involves, or is likely to lead to, the loss of more than 20 hectares of agricultural land of grades 1, 2 or 3a. This requirement is designed to ensure that they have the opportunity to comment on applications of this type. Further guidance on agricultural considerations and on the consultation arrangements is given in Annex A. Further advice in respect of mineral workings on agricultural land is included in MPGs.

Environmental assessment

2.7 An environmental statement will need to accompany a planning application where proposed development is of a type listed in Schedule 1 to the Town and Country Planning (Assessment of Environmental Effects) Regulations 1988 or is of a type listed in Schedule 2 and likely to have significant environmental effects. For any given proposal, the more environmentally sensitive the location, the more likely it is that environmental effects will be significant and that environmental assessment will be warranted. Further guidance on the environmental assessment provisions is given in DOE Circular 15/88 (Welsh Office 23/88), and in relation to SSSIs in DOE Circular 1/92 (Welsh Office 1/92).

Agricultural development

2.8 The total land area of England and Wales is about 15 million hectares. Over three quarters of this is used for farming. Another million hectares is woodland, and the use of land for woods and forestry is increasing. Agriculture in all its forms is likely to remain the land use that most influences the physical appearance and character of the countryside, even though significant areas of land are being taken out of agricultural use.

2.9 When the modern town and country planning system was introduced in 1947, boosting food production was a national priority, the pace of agricultural change was slow and the impact of agriculture on the countryside was seen as beneficial. Farming was therefore given a wide exemption from planning control. Although circumstances have changed, an efficient and flexible agricultural industry remains essential. While the Government has no plans to extend planning controls to all farming activities, it has been ready to introduce new closely-targeted controls over agricultural development where necessary to deal with specific problems.

AGRICULTURE is defined by section 336(1) of the Town and Country Planning Act 1990 as including:–

> *horticulture, fruit growing, seed growing, dairy farming, the breeding and keeping of livestock (including any creature kept for the production of food, wool, skins or furs, or the purpose of its use in the farming of land), the use of land as grazing land, meadow land, osier land, market gardens and nursery grounds, and the use of land for woodlands where that use is ancillary to the farming of land for other agricultural purposes.*

2.10   The use of land for the purposes of agriculture, and the use for those purposes of existing buildings on the land, do not constitute 'development' under section 55 of the Town and County Planning Act 1990 and so do not require planning permission. The construction, extension or alteration of a building, and the carrying out of excavations or engineering operations, do constitute 'development'. If this development is 'reasonably necessary for the purposes of agriculture', however, it may qualify as permitted development under the Town and Country Planning General Development Order and so not require specific planning permission. These permitted development rights are subject to various conditions. Developments that do not meet these conditions require planning permission in the usual way. Further guidance on planning controls over agricultural development is given in Annex B.

2.11   Under the Order, local planning authorities are able to regulate certain aspects of agricultural (and forestry) development for which full planning permission is not required. Where necessary, they may require details of new farm buildings, significant extensions and alterations (in National Parks, all extensions and alterations), farm roads, and certain excavations and waste deposits to be submitted for approval before work starts. Annex C provides guidance on these controls.

Rural businesses

2.12   The range of industries that can be successfully located in rural areas is expanding. Many commercial and light manufacturing activities can be carried on in rural areas without causing unacceptable disturbance. There are attractions to the firms and their staff in a clean and healthy environment, and there are benefits to the local economy and employment. These firms also help to bring new life and activity to rural communities, and so are generally welcomed and quickly assimilated. Local planning authorities should bear in mind the vital role of small scale enterprises in promoting a healthy rural economy. They should make provision in development plans, appropriate to the needs of the area, for commercial and

industrial development which can be accommodated without serious planning problems. Among the issues which authorities may wish to address in local plans is their policy towards the future expansion of business premises in the countryside.

2.13   In many rural areas, a lack of suitable workspace at affordable rent is holding back economic development. Re-use and adaptation of existing buildings (see paragraph 2.15) have an important role to play in meeting the demand for workspace. But provision needs to be made for new development as well. Sensitive, small-scale new development can be accommodated in and around many settlements. Structure plans should set out the overall strategy for such development. Local plans should provide a guide to the scale of allowable development and the criteria against which planning applications will be considered. In some villages, the pressure to convert existing buildings to dwellings is great, and applications for a change of use may, if granted, lead to adverse affects on the local rural economy. The need to accommodate local commerce and industry may well be a material consideration when deciding such applications.

Tourism, sport and recreation

2.14   Tourism plays an important part in the development and diversification of the rural economy, but can also damage the landscape and heritage on which it depends. Its growth needs to be reconciled with a full regard for the environment. A Planning Policy Guidance Note on tourism will be issued shortly. Advice on sport and recreation in the countryside is given in PPG17. When deciding planning applications authorities should take account of the effect of the proposed development on public rights of way. Footpaths and bridleways increase opportunities to enjoy the countryside.

Re-use and adaptation of rural buildings

2.15   There are often opportunities for re-using or adapting existing rural buildings for new commercial, industrial, or recreational uses. Such re-use or adaptation can help to reduce demands for new building in the countryside, can encourage new enterprises, and can provide jobs needed in rural areas. There should generally be no reason for preventing the re-use or adaptation of agricultural and other rural buildings for new uses, provided their form, bulk and general design are in keeping with their surroundings. Proposals for conversion of existing buildings may be more acceptable if they respect local building styles and materials.[1] Not all proposals will be acceptable since in some cases there may be legitimate objections, for example on environmental or traffic grounds, that outweigh the advantages of re-use. However, proposals for the re-use of such buildings should not be rejected unless there are specific and convincing planning reasons that cannot be overcome by attaching reasonable conditions to the planning permission. Planning authorities should bear in mind that the alternative to re-use may be a building that is left vacant and prone to vandalism and dereliction. Additional guidance on re-use and conversion is provided in Annex D.

[1] In accordance with Article 30 of the Treaty of Rome, conditions should not rule out the use of equivalent natural materials that are not local.

Housing

2.16 New housing will continue to be required in rural areas, to sustain the health of the rural economy and the viability of village communities. In many villages provision can be made for modest development without damage to the character of the village or to the countryside. New housing can help to sustain villages by providing the basis for maintaining local services, schools, shops, pubs and other features of community life.

2.17 Changes in the area of land devoted to farming mean that it should be possible to accommodate small-scale new housing development more readily in rural areas, and to secure more generous and imaginative standards of lay-out and landscape design. It is nevertheless still important that the pattern of new development should be determined through the development plan process, and should be well related in scale and location to existing development. Expansion of villages and towns must avoid creating ribbon development or a fragmented pattern of development.

2.18 New housebuilding and other new development in the open countryside, away from established settlements, should be strictly controlled. The fact that a single house on a particular site would be unobtrusive is not by itself a good argument; it could be repeated too often. Isolated new houses in the countryside require special justification – for example, where they are essential to enable farm or forestry workers to live at or near their place of work. Advice on the special considerations which may arise in relation to agricultural and forestry dwellings is given in Annex E. Infilling (the filling of small gaps within small groups of houses) or minor extensions to groups may be acceptable. Much would depend on the character of the surroundings and the number of such groups in the area.

2.19 In an increasing number of rural areas there are pressures on the limited housing stock from people outside the local community. Some will bring new businesses and skills to rural areas but others will include retired people and long-distance commuters. Many can afford to pay more for their housing than local people. The result can be a serious shortage of affordable housing for those with modest incomes who already live and work in the area. Advice on the provision of land to meet local needs for affordable housing (in areas where new housing would normally be permitted and elsewhere) and on arrangements for ensuring that the benefits are passed to successive occupants, is given in DOE Circular 7/91 (Welsh Office 31/91).

2.20 Planning Policy Guidance Note 3 provides advice on the identification and allocation of land for housing in England. Advice on the provision of land for housing in Wales is given in Welsh Office Circular 47/84.

Horses

2.21 The keeping and riding of horses for recreational purposes or as part of commercially-based equestrian activities is increasingly popular in many parts of the countryside, not least those close to urban areas. Such activities can help provide new opportunities for employment and land use. Guidance on development involving horses is provided in Annex F.

3. Special considerations in designated areas

Introduction

3.1 In those parts of the countryside where special statutory designations apply planning policies and development control decisions should take full account of the specific features or qualities which justified designation of the area, and sustain or further the purposes of that designation. In some designated areas additional statutory planning controls or procedures apply, for example through tighter controls over permitted development. Other designations have statutory implications beyond the planning system, but the factors that led to the designation may also be material to planning decisions.

Permitted development rights in designated areas

Permitted development rights allow a range of minor developments to take place without the need for a full planning permission requiring a planning application.

In National Parks and the Broads, AONBs and conservation areas some permitted development right are reduced, and others withdrawn entirely, so that some types of normally minor development remain subject to scrutiny by the planning system. There are lower volume limits for the extension of dwellinghouses, and for the erection of buildings within the curtilage of dwellinghouses. Extensions to industrial buildings and warehouses that can be undertaken without specific planning permission are subject to lower volume and floorspace allowances. Permitted development rights are not available at all for:

- roof extensions to dwellinghouses;

- the application of stone and some other forms of cladding to the outside of a dwellinghouse;

- the installation of a satellite dish on chimney stacks and on walls or roof-slopes fronting a highway (or a waterway in the Broads) as well as on buildings over 15 metres in height; or

National Parks and Areas of Outstanding Natural Beauty in England and Wales

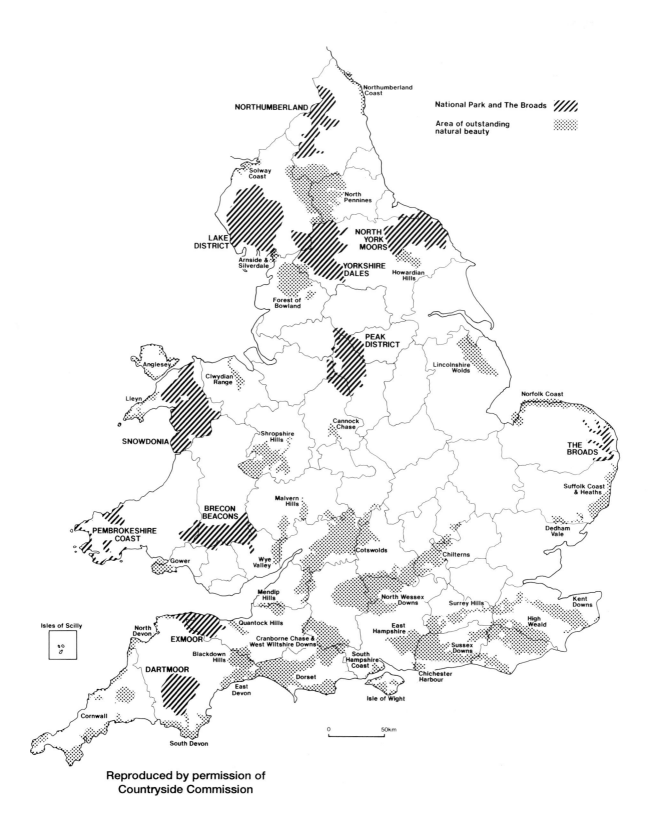

National Park and The Broads

Area of outstanding natural beauty

Northumberland Coast

NORTHUMBERLAND

Solway Coast

North Pennines

LAKE DISTRICT

NORTH YORK MOORS

Arnside & Silverdale

YORKSHIRE DALES

Howardian Hills

Forest of Bowland

PEAK DISTRICT

Anglesey

Clwydian Range

Lincolnshire Wolds

Lleyn

Norfolk Coast

SNOWDONIA

Shropshire Hills

Cannock Chase

THE BROADS

Suffolk Coast & Heaths

Malvern Hills

BRECON BEACONS

Cotswolds

Chilterns

Dedham Vale

PEMBROKESHIRE COAST

Wye Valley

Kent Downs

Gower

Mendip Hills

North Wessex Downs

Surrey Hills

High Weald

Isles of Scilly

North Devon

Quantock Hills

EXMOOR

Cranborne Chase & West Wiltshire Downs

East Hampshire

Sussex Downs

Blackdown Hills

DARTMOOR

South Hampshire Coast

Chichester Harbour

Dorset

Cornwall

East Devon

Isle of Wight

0   50km

South Devon

Reproduced by permission of
Countryside Commission

– the installation or alteration of a microwave antenna by a "code systems operator" licensed under the Telecommunications Act 1984. Operators must also give the local planning authority prior notification of their intention to install apparatus.

In National Parks and the Broads permitted development rights are not available for fish farm excavations and engineering operations and all proposals to extend or alter an agricultural building under permitted development rights may be subject to controls over siting and design.

National Parks

3.2 National Parks are designated by the Countryside Commission and the Countryside Council for Wales, subject to confirmation by the Secretaries of State, under the National Parks and Access to the Countryside Act 1949. The statutory purposes of National Parks are conservation of the natural beauty of the countryside and promotion of its public enjoyment. (PPG17, Sport and Recreation, makes clear that where there is an irreconcilable conflict between these purposes conservation must take precedence over recreation.) Under the Countryside Act 1968, National Park Authorities are required to have due regard to the economic and social interests of their areas. There are seven National Parks in England and three in Wales covering a total of 13,600 square kilometres, which is 9 per cent of the total land area of England and Wales (see map). In April 1989, the Norfolk and Suffolk Broads Act 1988 brought the Broads Authority into being. The Broads have the same status as a National Park and the Broads Authority exercises in its area similar functions to those of the National Park Authorities.

3.3 The Broads Authority has had local plan making powers since its inception. The Government has recognised that for consistency of policy making each National Park should be considered in its entirety and that responsibility for detailed planning in National Parks should rest with the National Park Authorities. The Planning and Compensation Act 1991 requires National Park Authorities to prepare a local plan covering the whole of their areas, as well as minerals and waste policies. National Parks and the Broads will continue to be covered by the appropriate county structure plans, except for the Lake District and Peak District which are responsible for the structure plans for their areas.

3.4 National Park Authorities and the Broads Authority determine planning applications on the basis of the policies in their local plans. These policies may be supplemented by more detailed guidance on appropriate materials or design for new developments or extensions to existing buildings. Such guidance should be given wide publicity.

3.5 National Park Authorities and the Broads Authority are responsible for development control in their areas. In the National Parks, planning applications are now made directly to National Park Authorities for decision. Planning applications in the Broads Authority area will continue to be submitted to the district council in which the proposed development lies, who pass applications to the Authority for decision.

3.6 Conservation of the natural beauty of the countryside should be given great weight in planning policies and development control decisions in the National Parks and the Broads. Due regard should also be had to the economic and social well-being of the area. Special considerations apply to major development proposals, which are more national than local in character. Major development should not take place in the National Parks and the Broads save in exceptional circumstances. Because of the serious impact that major developments may have on their natural beauty, applications for such developments must be subject to the most rigorous examination. Unlike the position elsewhere in England and Wales, major developments should be demonstrated to be in the public interest before being allowed to proceed. Consideration of such applications should therefore normally include an assessment of:

(i) the need for the development, in terms of national considerations, and the impact of permitting it or refusing it upon the local economy;

(ii) the cost of and scope for developing elsewhere outside the area or meeting the need for it in some other way;

(iii) any detrimental effect on the environment and the landscape, and the extent to which that should be moderated.

Any construction or restoration should be carried out to high environmental standards. These tests are based on those already applied to minerals development in the National Parks. The Government is currently reviewing Minerals Planning Guidance notes 1 and 6.

3.7 Advice on environmental assessment is given in paragraph 2.7. In National Parks and the Broads a greater proportion of Schedule 2 proposals may require environmental assessment than in the wider countryside, because of possible effects on conservation and opportunities for public enjoyment. There is no statutory provision on the form of an environmental assessment but National Park Authorities and the Broads Authority may reasonably expect a prospective developer to address the issue of the impact of his proposal on their purposes and to place more explicit emphasis on the consideration of alternative options.

Areas of Outstanding Natural Beauty

3.8 AONBs are designated by the same means and under the same legislation as National Parks.

There are 39 designated AONBs in England and Wales (see map), covering a total of 20,400 square kilometres – around 13 per cent of the total land area. The primary objective of designation is conservation of the natural beauty of the landscape. This objective should be reflected by local authorities in their preparation of structure and local plans and exercise of development control. AONBs differ from National Parks in that the promotion of recreation is not an objective of their designation, though these areas should be used to meet the demand for recreation so far as that is consistent with the conservation of natural beauty and the needs of agriculture, forestry and other uses. There are no special statutory arrangements for the administration of AONBs although the Government endorses the practice of setting up joint advisory committees to bring together both local authorities and amenity groups, farming and other interests to encourage a coordinated approach to their management. This will be especially important where AONBs cover the area of several local authorities, who will wish to ensure that their policies are broadly compatible.

3.9 In general, policies and development control decisions affecting AONBs should favour conservation of the natural beauty of the landscape. In all cases the environmental effects of new proposals will be a major consideration, though it will also be appropriate to have regard to the economic and social well-being of the areas. It would normally be inconsistent with the aims of designation to permit the siting of major industrial or commercial development in these areas. Only proven national interest and lack of alternative sites can justify an exception.

3.10 Applications for new mineral workings, or extensions to existing works, in AONBs must be subject to the most rigorous examination. If permission is granted, it should be subject to appropriate standards of operation, restoration and aftercare. Further advice is given in Minerals Planning Guidance notes.

3.11 Similar considerations apply to proposals for new road construction. The methods of assessment used to appraise trunk road proposals already take account of their impact on the landscape, but schemes affecting AONBs should be examined with particular care to ensure that a new road is needed and that the route and design chosen do as little damage to the environment as practicable.

Green Belts and the urban fringe

3.12 Green Belts are established through development plans, to check urban sprawl, safeguard the surrounding countryside, prevent neighbouring towns from merging, preserve the special character of historic towns, and assist urban regeneration. They cover some 15,500 square kilometres, about 12% of England. There are none in Wales. Within Green Belts there is, in addition to the general policies controlling development in the countryside, a presumption against inappropriate development. Policy on Green Belts is set out in PPG2.

3.13 Despite the strict control of urban sprawl there are around some conurbations areas of "urban fringe" where land use conflicts and environmental problems arise. Urban fringe is *not* a designation, though some urban fringe areas are found within Green Belts. The urban fringe often accommodates essential but unneighbourly functions such as waste disposal and sewage treatment, and contains areas of derelict land and damaged landscape and under-used land whose viability for agricultural use has been affected by urban pressures. It requires a positive approach to planning and management, aimed at securing environmental improvement and beneficial use of land, and increased public access, to provide an amenity for the residents of urban areas.

Sites of Special Scientific Interest

3.14 SSSIs are designated by English Nature and the Countryside Council for Wales under section 28 of the Wildlife and Countryside Act 1981. To date some 4,300 sites, covering a total of 9,750 square kilometres, have been designated in England and Wales. SSSIs cover 6.5 per cent of England and Wales; some are located in National Parks, AONBs or Green Belts. Sites are identified on the basis of published scientific criteria and their designation is intended to protect the nature conservation interest of the site. Some SSSIs are also subject to an additional designation in recognition of their special nature conservation interest: National Nature Reserves, designated by the nature conservation agencies under the Wildlife and Countryside Act 1981, are reserves considered to be of national importance; 'Ramsar' sites, selected by the agencies and designated by the Secretary of State, are wetlands of international importance, especially for waterfowl, under the Ramsar Convention of 1971; and Special Protection Areas, also selected by the agencies and designated by the Secretary of State, are areas for the protection of rare and migratory birds under the European Community Wild Birds Directive (79/409). Advice on planning and nature conservation is provided in DOE Circulars 27/87 and 1/92 (Welsh Office 52/87 and 1/92); a PPG on nature conservation will be issued shortly.

Historic and archaeological sites

3.15 The countryside contains a large number of historic buildings and areas, some of which are covered by additional controls. Advice on listed buildings and conservation areas is set out in DOE Circular 8/87 (Welsh Office 61/81). Conservation areas are designated as areas of special architectural or historic interest, in which local authorities must pay special attention to the desirability of preserving or enhancing their character or appearance in exercising their planning powers. A number of conservation areas are found in villages, while some cover parkland around historic buildings. English Heritage maintain a non-statutory register of gardens and other land in England which they consider to be of historic interest, to aid authorities and developers in planning new development. In Wales, CADW are in the process of compiling a similar register.

3.16 The countryside is also rich in the remains of human activity over thousands of years. Some archaeological remains or sites of national importance are designated by the Secretary of State as scheduled monuments under the Ancient Monuments and Archaeological Areas Act 1979. Any works which might damage them require the prior consent of the Secretary of State. The desirability of preserving an ancient monument and its setting is a material consideration, whether or not that monument is scheduled. Advice on archaeology and planning is in PPG 16; there are separate versions for England and for Wales.

Other designations

3.17 There are further designations, applied to other areas of the countryside, which have no direct statutory implications for the planning process, for example in terms of any limitation of permitted development rights or the need for formal consultation with specific interests, but which nevertheless serve to highlight particularly important features of the countryside that should be taken into account in planning decisions. These include locally-devised ones, such as Areas of Great Landscape Value, which local planning authorities sometimes include in their structure or local plans to denote areas to which special countryside protection or other policies apply.

Environmentally Sensitive Areas

3.18 Environmentally Sensitive Areas are designated by agriculture departments in England and Wales under the Agriculture Act 1986 and particular policies and programmes apply within them. ESAs (see map) are areas of special landscape, wildlife or historic interest which can be protected or enhanced by supporting specific agricultural practices. Designation as an ESA does not affect the status of the area in terms of national planning policies or development control regulations. However, the features which contributed to the designation of the area as an ESA may sometimes also be important features in local countryside planning policies and development control decisions.

4 Cancellations

4.1 This Planning Policy Guidance note is an expanded and updated version of the first edition of PPG7, published in January 1988. The first edition of PPG7, the Annex to DOE Circular 24/73 (Welsh Office 49/73), DOE Circular 16/87 (Welsh Office 25/87) and Development Control Policy Note 4 (Development in Rural Areas, 1969) are hereby cancelled.

Environmentally Sensitive Areas

■ Existing ESAs

▨ Proposed ESAs

The extent of the proposed ESA's is illustrative not definitive.

Lake District

Pennine Dales

North Peak

South West Peak

Lleyn Peninsula

Shropshire Hills

Shropshire Borders

Cambrian Mountains

Cotswold Hills

Breckland

Broads

Suffolk River Valleys

Essex Coast

Upper Thames Tributaries

North West Kent Coast

Somerset Levels and Moors

North Dorset / South Wilts Downs

Test Valley

South Downs

Exmoor

Blackdown Hills

Hampshire Avon

Dartmoor

West Penwith

0   100

Kilometres

Crown Copyright 1991

ANNEX A: DEVELOPMENT INVOLVING AGRICULTURAL LAND

AGRICULTURAL CONSIDERATIONS

Agricultural land quality

A1   To assist in assessing land quality, MAFF has classified agricultural land by grade according to the extent to which its physical or chemical characteristics impose long term limitations on agricultural use for food production. The MAFF Agricultural Land Classification (ALC) system classifies land into five grades numbered 1 to 5, with grade 3 divided into two sub-grades (3a and 3b). The system was devised and introduced in the 1960s. Revised technical guidelines and criteria for grading using this system were published in 1988, under the title "Agricultural Land Classification of England and Wales". These guidelines update the system without changing the original concepts.

A2   The best and most versatile agricultural land falls into grades 1 and 2 and sub-grade 3a. This land ranges from excellent (grade 1) to good quality (sub-grade 3a) and is the most flexible, productive and efficient in response to inputs. It is thus best suited to adapting to the changing needs of agriculture and maintaining the competitiveness of UK agriculture vis a vis our international competitors. Such land collectively comprises about one third of the agricultural land in England and Wales.

A3   Land in sub-grade 3b is of moderate quality with lower yields and/or a more restricted cropping range. Grades 4 and 5 are poor and very poor quality land with severe or very severe limitations respectively.

A4   Proposed changes to the use of the best and most versatile land are the most significant in terms of the national agricultural interest. Changes to land in sub-grade 3b or grades 4 or 5 would not normally be opposed on agricultural land quality grounds although in some areas, especially the hills and uplands, 3b and 4 land can have special importance for the rural economy and management of individual farms.

A5   ALC maps at a scale of 1" to 1 mile were published in the late 1960s and early 1970s covering the whole of England and Wales. The information is also published at a reduced scale of 1:250,000. These reconnaissance maps were produced for use in strategic planning and therefore provide only a generalised indication of the distribution of land quality, as recorded at the time of survey. The maps are not suitable for use in evaluating individual sites where development is proposed. In such cases a resurvey at a larger scale is necessary to obtain a definitive grade.

A6   The above ALC maps and in some cases the associated reports and the publication "Agricultural Land Classification of England and Wales" can be purchased from MAFF Publications, Deptford, London SE99 7TP. ALC maps for specific areas at larger scales may also be available.

Other factors

A7   *The location of development in relation to farms* – The proximity of other development to farms, and its nature, can influence the type of farming and the extent to which inherent land quality can be exploited. Certain locations may have agricultural advantages such as the accessibility to markets, processing plant and certain industries associated with agriculture. Conversely, farms with development close to them tend to suffer from tresspass and other forms of disturbance which may affect the efficiency and upkeep of holdings. It may be possible to reduce any detrimental effects of development by locating compatible uses adjacent to farm land, by landscaping or by detailed provision in the layout of residential development.

A8   *Farm size and structure* – Farms vary considerably in size, type of farm business and layout. The loss of part of a holding can have important implications for the remainder. The effect of severance and fragmentation upon the farm and its structure may be relevant.

A9   *Buildings and other fixed equipment* – The efficiency of farms can be affected by the conditions and extent of buildings and other fixed equipment. The full use of these assets could be impaired by the loss of specific sites to development and there may be proposals to improve buildings and equipment which are tied to investment decisions already taken. The effect on the capital investment of a farm should, therefore, be taken into account as part of the consideration of the agricultural case.

A10   *Other effects of development on agriculture* – In addition to the factors referred to above development may have further consequences for agriculture. For example, it may be necessary to redesign land drainage systems disturbed by development and, where major development is involved, the drainage of surface water may require water courses to be re-aligned or improved to accept the increased flow. Freshwater and marine fisheries may be affected by discharges from industrial and other forms of development. Where statutory allotments are to be developed, MAFF can advise on the suitability of alternative land for allotments.

PROCEDURAL ARRANGEMENTS FOR CONSULTATION WITH THE MINISTRY OF AGRICULTURE, FISHERIES AND FOOD AND THE WELSH OFFICE AGRICULTURE DEPARTMENT

Consultation on development plans and Strategic and Regional Guidance

A11   Local planning authorities preparing development plans or alterations to such plans under the Town and Country Planning Act 1990 are advised to consult Government Departments where plan proposals appear to affect their interests. Local planning authorities preparing plans should therefore continue to consult MAFF (in Wales, WOAD) and other Government Departments where appropriate. PPG12 on development plans and regional planning guidance gives further guidance. MAFF will continue to offer comment as they consider necessary on the preparation of plans. MAFF will also continue to advise local planning authorities on the relative quality of agricultural land in the plan area and on identifying the best and most versatile land. The Secretary of State will consult MAFF when preparing or revising Strategic Guidance or Regional Planning Guidance.

A12 Section 44(3) of the Town and Country Planning Act 1990 gives MAFF a statutory right to require that the Secretary of State should call in local plans to which MAFF continue to object. Under Section 18(3) of the Act MAFF have similar rights in respect of unitary development plans. These rights will continue to be exercised only in the most exceptional circumstances.

Consultation on individual planning applications for non-agricultural development

A13 There may from time to time be proposals for development for non-agricultural purposes requiring significant amounts of higher quality agricultural land. In such cases MAFF have the statutory right to be consulted, so that local planning authorities are made fully aware of the agricultural implications. Article 18(v) of the Town and Country Planning General Development Order 1988 requires the local planning authority to consult the Minister of Agriculture, Fisheries and Food (in Wales, the Secretary of State for Wales) before granting any planning application which is not in accordance with the development plan, and would involve (i) the loss of 20 hectares or more of grades 1, 2 or 3a agricultural land or (ii) a loss which is less than 20 hectares but is likely to lead to further losses amounting cumulatively to 20 hectares or more. If the local planning authority are uncertain whether the land involved is grades 1, 2 or 3a they may seek advice from MAFF on its classification.

A14 Irrespective of the size of the site, or the land quality, under Schedule 5 of the Town and Country Planning Act 1990 (as amended) MAFF will be consulted on aftercare conditions where land is to be returned to agricultural use following planning permission involving minerals working or the depositing of minerals waste and any type of refuse or waste material. The statutory requirement for consulting MAFF on agricultural aftercare does not apply to planning conditions governing the restoration of the land by the use of soil materials. However, it is clear that the achievement of good standards in the aftercare period must in part depend on appropriate (and enforced) planning conditions, covering, for example, the stripping and movement of soils and their restoration on appropriate contoured ground

after minerals extraction. MAFF will therefore continue to comment or advise on restoration conditions. Minerals planning authorities will need to receive such comments concurrently with the advice under Schedule 5. The arrangements outlined in paragraph A13 above will however apply to minerals planning authorities in the same way as they apply to other local planning authorities. Further advice on agricultural restoration and aftercare of minerals workings is contained in Minerals Planning Guidance note 7, The Reclamation of Mineral Workings.

Non-statutory consultation with MAFF: non-agricultural development

A15 There may be other planning applications with significant agricultural implications which come to the attention of MAFF but which are not subject to the statutory requirements described in paragraphs A13 and A14 above. MAFF may on occasion wish to take the initiative in commenting to the local planning authority on applications of this type.

A16 In circumstances which do not require the specific consultations with MAFF outlined in paragraph A13 above it is expected that local authorities should normally be able to determine applications for development on agricultural land in the light of the evidence before them. Where they do not feel able to determine the application satisfactorily, it is open to them to seek more information or technical advice, eg as to the agricultural land quality of the land or other agricultural implications, either from MAFF or from other agricultural consultants. Such consultations should however be confined to matters of technical detail and not relate to the merits or otherwise of the application, on which it is for the local planning authority to take a view.

A17 In addition, when a planning application is submitted for "hard" development on former agricultural land of grades 1, 2 or 3a, which has previously been developed for a use which would allow the land to be returned to agriculture, the local planning authority should consult MAFF about the proposals.

Non-statutory consultation with MAFF: agricultural development

A18 This PPG provides comprehensive guidance to help authorities dealing with applications for agricultural development and agricultural dwellinghouses. Local planning authorities should generally be able to determine planning applications satisfactorily on the basis of this advice and the information before them. If this is not the case, MAFF will be prepared to give a technical appraisal on specific points; this will be confined to a factual statement of the agricultural considerations involved and an evaluation of the specific matters on which advice is sought, but will make no recommendation for or against the application. Agricultural consultants may also be able to give advice. MAFF will charge for technical appraisals in relation to all applications for agricultural development including the lifting of agricultural occupancy conditions.

Refusal of permission or imposition of planning conditions for agricultural reasons

A19   When any views expressed by MAFF are material to the refusal of planning permission, or to the imposition of conditions on a permission granted, it will be necessary for the authority to refer to them in their notice of decision, in accordance with the provisions of Article 25(ii) of the General Development Order. Where, apart from any views expressed by the Minister or the Secretary of State for Wales, agricultural considerations are a reason for refusal of planning permission this should be stated in the notice of decision in the usual way.

Appeals

A20   It will be open to the Secretary of State, or in cases decided by Inspectors to the Inspector, to ask MAFF to provide a technical appraisal if he considers this necessary to ensure that agricultural issues are fully covered in the course of an appeal. Such a technical appraisal would be made available to the parties on the same basis as if it had been requested by the local planning authority at the application stage.

Pre-inquiry statements and representation at inquiries

A21   Where an application is called-in for the Secretary of State's determination or goes to appeal, and a local inquiry is to be held, the Town and Country Planning Inquiries Procedure Rules apply. These provide that, where MAFF have expressed to the local planning authority a view that permission should not be granted, either wholly or in part, or should only be granted subject to conditions:

- MAFF will be informed by the authority of the inquiry and should, unless they have already done so, give a written statement of the reasons for their view;

- the authority must include the terms of MAFF's expression of view in their pre-inquiry statement of case; and

- the appellant will be able to require MAFF to provide a representative at the inquiry.

These arrangements apply whether or not the consultation with MAFF has been carried out under statutory arrangements. The authority may also wish to ask MAFF to be represented at an inquiry.

ANNEX B: PLANNING CONTROLS OVER AGRICULTURAL DEVELOPMENT

Permitted development rights for agricultural holdings

B1.1   Part 6 of Schedule 2 to the Town and Country Planning General Development Order grants permitted development rights for a range of agricultural buildings and operations. Rights for erecting, extending or altering a building, and for excavations and engineering operations, are available to agricultural units of at least 5 hectares under *Class A*. More limited rights, including extensions and alterations adding not more than 10% to the content of the original building, are available to smaller units of at least 0.4 hectare under *Class B*.

B1.2   Class A rights are not available on separate parcels of land of less than 1 hectare, while Class B rights are not available on separate parcels of less than 0.4 hectare. Parcels may be separated from the rest of the unit by, for example, land in different ownership or a public road. The rights are subject to various other limitations and conditions, the most important of which are mentioned below.

B1.3   Under both Classes, development:

– must be on agricultural land, which means land in use for agriculture for the purposes of a trade or business, and excludes any dwellinghouse or garden;

– must be reasonably necessary for the purposes of agriculture within the unit. This condition does not require that a new building should necessarily accommodate an agricultural use already existing in the unit. Agricultural developments which are entirely self-contained and have no direct relationship with the rest of the unit may thus benefit from permitted development rights;

– must not give rise to, or alter or extend, a dwelling;

– must not be within 25 metres of the metalled part of a trunk or classified road.

B1.4   Under *Class A*:

– development giving rise to buildings, structures or works not designed for agricultural purposes is not permitted. The courts have held that this condition relates to the physical appearance and layout of a building, not its function;

– buildings, structures or works must not exceed 12 metres in height, or 3 metres within 3 kilometres of the perimeter of an aerodrome;

– the ground area of any works or structure (other than a fence) for accommodating livestock or any plant and machinery arising from engineering operations, or of any building erected or extended under this Class, must not exceed 465 square metres. The relevant calculation is: (i) the ground area of the proposed development;

plus (ii) the ground area of any building (other than a dwelling), structure, works, plant, machinery, ponds or tanks which is (a) within the same agricultural unit, (b) less than 2 years old, and (c) within 90 metres of the proposed development.   Hardstandings   should   be included in (i) only if they are for accommodating livestock, but in (ii) whether or not they are so used;

– there are restrictions on livestock units and stores for slurry and sewage sludge located near 'protected buildings' (see paragraphs B3.1 and B3.2 below);

– development consisting of the significant extension or significant alteration of a building may be carried out only once. Any extension or alteration where the cubic content of the original building would be exceeded by more than 10%, or the height of the original building would be exceeded, is defined as "significant";

– local planning authorities may require their prior approval to be obtained for details of new buildings, significant extensions and alterations (or in National Parks and some adjoining areas – which are known in the GDO as Article 1(6) land – all extensions and alterations), farm roads, and certain excavations and waste deposits (see Annex C).

B1.5   *Class B* rights are subject to the limitation that the external appearance of the premises must not be materially affected. There are similar limitations   on   developments   for   livestock   and slurry/sewage sludge to those under Class A. Extensions and alterations to agricultural buildings:

– must not increase the height of the building;

– must not increase the cubic content of the original building by more than 10%;

– must not bring the ground area of the building to more than 465 square metres;

– on Article 1(6) land are subject to the same conditions concerning prior approval of details as extensions and alterations under Class A.

B1.6   Rights are also available under Class B for certain development in connection with private ways, for apparatus such as sewers and cables, for certain waste deposits, and – subject to limitations on area – for additional or replacement plant or machinery and for hard surfaces. The details of private ways are subject to the prior approval conditions on Article 1(6) land. Any plant or machinery must not exceed 12 metres in height (or 3 metres within 3 kilometres of the perimeter of an aerodrome), and in any case replacement plant and machinery must not exceed the height of what it replaces. Waste deposits must not materially increase the height of the land.

B1.7   *Fish farming* for food can benefit from the permitted development rights available under Classes A and B. However under Class A:

- on Article 1(6) land no rights are available for excavations or engineering operations connected with fish farming;

- elsewhere the placing or assembly of a fish tank (defined to include a cage or other structure for use in fish farming) in any waters is permitted subject to the prior approval conditions;

and under Class B:

- certain rights specific to fish farming are available in connection with repair and maintenance and installing equipment;

- development is not permitted if it involves the placing or assembly of a fish tank on land or in any waters, the construction of a fish pond, or an increase in the size of a fish tank or pond (except by removing silt).

B1.8 The definition of livestock in Classes A and B includes fish. Fish farm excavations which exceed 0.5 hectare, when added to other excavations and waste deposits on the unit, are subject to the prior approval conditions under Class A.

B1.9 The GDO requires local planning authorities to consult the National Rivers Authority before granting permission for development for the purposes of fish farming (whether for food or for any other purpose).

Farm shops and workshops

B2 It is normally assumed that use of a farm shop only for the sale of goods produced on that farm is a use which is ancillary to the use as a farm and therefore does not require specific planning permission, whereas use as a farm shop selling a significant amount of 'imported' produce is a separate use and therefore subject to full planning control. Similar considerations apply to workshops for the central maintenance of agricultural equipment.

Livestock units and slurry

B3.1 Permitted development rights under Part 6 of the GDO do not extend to buildings to be used for the accommodation of livestock, or to associated structures such as slurry tanks and lagoons, when these are to be built within 400 metres of the curtilage of a 'protected building'. This applies to new buildings and structures, to ones created by the conversion of other farm buildings and structures erected under Part 6 since 2 January 1992, and to ones extended or altered under Class B. These may however be used for livestock in special circumstances (as defined in paragraph D.3 of Part 6 of the GDO). A full planning application is required for the livestock use of buildings and structures erected within the 400 metre cordon under Part 6 between 1988 and 1 January 1992, unless they were completed more than five years ago.

B3.2. The term 'protected building' includes most residential and other permanent buildings such as schools, hospitals and offices that are normally occupied by people. It excludes any building on the same agricultural unit, any farm dwelling or other farm building on another agricultural unit, and any building used for the special industrial uses covered by Classes B3–B7 of the Use Classes Order 1987. The 400 metres will usually be measured from the boundary of the land on which the 'protected building' stands – for example, from the end of the garden of a house.

B3.3 To minimise the potential for future conflict between neighbouring land uses, local planning authorities should exercise particular care when considering planning applications for houses or other new 'protected' buildings within 400 metres of established livestock units. By requiring planning permission for livestock units within the 400 metre cordon, the Government has recognised the potential risk of nuisance. This recognition should similarly apply to applications for new protected buildings. It is important also to have regard to the advice on not siting incompatible development close to animal waste processing factories in DOE Circular 43/76 (Welsh Office 17/76, MAFF 76/CSAWP/1), Control of smells from the animal waste processing industry.

B3.4 The spreading of slurry from livestock units for the purposes of agriculture is not subject to planning control. It remains important, however, to minimise the risk that such activities may cause nuisance from noise or smell. Accordingly, those responsible for the operation of livestock units should follow the advice given in the new code of good agricultural practice for the protection of water published by the Ministry of Agriculture, Fisheries and Food and the Welsh Office Agriculture Department, and further codes relating to the protection of air and soil which should be published in 1992.

B3.5 The Control of Pollution (Silage, Slurry and Agricultural Fuel Oil) Regulations 1991 set minimum standards for new, substantially reconstructed or enlarged silage, slurry or fuel oil facilities. The Regulations also empower the National Rivers Authority to serve notice requiring action to improve existing installations when they consider that there is a significant risk of pollution. Further guidance on these regulations is contained in "The Control of Pollution (Silage, Slurry and Agricultural Fuel Oil) Regulations 1991; Guidance Notes for Farmers" prepared by the Department of the Environment and the Welsh Office. These Regulations form an important part of the Government's commitment to reduce agricultural pollution of rivers. Local planning authorities are therefore encouraged to consider sympathetically development proposals aimed at meeting the requirements of these Regulations.

B3.6 Local planning authorities should in general adopt a positive approach towards development proposals which are designed, or are necessary, to achieve compliance with new environmental, hygiene and welfare legislation. For example, the Welfare of Pigs Regulations 1991 prohibit the installation of stall and tether systems from 1 October 1991 and ban the use of these systems altogether from 1 January 1999. Currently, up to 70% of sows in the UK are housed in stall and tether systems. Farmers using these close confinement systems are likely to need to double the space allocation for sows and provide extra storage space for bedding straw and solid manure. Planning applications for associated building development may therefore be necessary.

Temporary structures

B4   The Courts have held that some temporary structures used for agriculture are not 'buildings' in planning terms but are a use of land and so outside the general scope of planning control. Thus, temporary accommodation for livestock, such as 'pig arks' and moveable poultry shelters, may not be 'buildings' for planning purposes. The status of particular structures is ultimately a matter for the Courts to decide, on the facts of each case. A structure placed on foundations, secured to the ground and with, for example, facilities such as an integral water supply may constitute a building, while a structure without such features may constitute a use of land. In case of doubt an application may be made to the local planning authority for a determination under section 64 of the Town and Country Planning Act 1990 as to whether planning permission is required. (The Planning and Compensation Act 1991 provides for section 64 to be repealed and section 192 to be amended; when these provisions are brought into effect later in 1992, application may be made under section 192 for a certificate of lawfulness of proposed use or development.)

Central grain stores

B5.1   Central grain stores are large agricultural buildings used as collection and distribution points for the produce of several farms. The UK is a net exporter of grain and it is important that the harvest is handled and marketed to the best advantage nationally. The advantages of central grain stores for the farmers concerned are that equipment for drying, cleaning, and preparing grain may be operated at lower cost than on individual farms, that different types or qualities of grain can be assembled separately, and that they are suitably located relative to the main grain growing areas and/or docks. Such buildings also enable grain to be stored near where it is to be processed. As older on-farm stores are due for replacement, more growers wish to use centralised storage that meets modern marketing requirements.

B5.2 In view of their potentially obtrusive appearance, central grain stores should be designed and located with particular care to minimise their effect on the landscape. In considering applications for central grain stores local planning authorities should have regard to the advantages of such stores, as indicated above, as well as the extent to which they blend with their surroundings and traffic and other relevant planning considerations. In some instances it may be possible to locate new central grain stores in industrial areas on the edge of settlements rather than in open countryside.

ANNEX C: GUIDANCE FOR LOCAL PLANNING AUTHORITIES ON AGRICULTURAL AND FORESTRY BUILDINGS AND ROADS CONSTRUCTED UNDER PERMITTED DEVELOPMENT RIGHTS

Introduction

C1   The Town and Country Planning General Development Order 1988, as amended, grants planning permission for a wide range of development associated with agricultural uses of land, on units of 5 hectares or more, and forestry uses of land. However, in certain cases this planning permission cannot be exercised unless the farmer or other developer has applied to the local planning authority for a determination as to whether their prior approval will be required for certain details. The local planning authority have 28 days for initial consideration of the proposed development. Within this period they may decide whether or not it is necessary for them to give their prior approval to these details of development involving new agricultural and forestry buildings, significant extensions and alterations, agricultural and forestry roads, certain excavations or waste deposits, and the placing or assembly of fish tanks in any waters. In National Parks and certain adjoining areas ('Article 1(6) land'), *all* extensions and alterations to buildings are subject to this procedure and the placing or assembly of fish tanks in any waters requires a specific planning application to be made to the local planning authority.

C2   The amended Order also grants planning permission for strictly limited types of development on smaller agricultural units of less than 5 hectares (but no smaller than 0.4 hectare). These types of development are not subject to the determination procedure, except on Article 1(6) land, where the procedure applies to extensions and alterations of buildings and the provision, rearrangement or replacement of roads.

C3   These provisions are in Parts 6 and 7 of Schedule 2 to the General Development Order. The determination procedure provides planning authorities with a means of regulating, where necessary, important aspects of agricultural and forestry development for which full planning permission is not required by virtue of the GDO. Provided all the GDO requirements are met, the principle of whether the development should be permitted is not for consideration. Only in cases where the authority considers that a specific proposal is likely to have a significant impact on its surroundings would the Secretaries of State consider it necessary for the authority to require the formal submission of details for approval. By no means all the development proposals notified to authorities under the GDO will have such an impact. Indeed there is no statutory requirement for the authority to take any action when they

receive the developer's written description unless they consider it appropriate.

C4   In operating these controls, local authorities should always have full regard to the operational needs of the agricultural and forestry industries; to the need to avoid imposing any unnecessary or excessively costly requirements; and to the normal considerations of reasonableness. However, they will also need to consider the effect of the development on the landscape in terms of visual amenity and the desirability of preserving ancient monuments and their settings, known archaeological sites, listed buildings and their settings, and sites of recognised nature conservation value. They should weigh these two sets of considerations. Long term conservation objectives will often be served best by ensuring that the rural economy, including farming and forestry which are prominent in the rural landscape, is able to function successfully.

Handling

C5   The 28 day determination period runs from the date of receipt of the written description of the proposed development by the local planning authority. If the local planning authority give notice that prior approval is required they will then have the normal 8 week period from the receipt of the submitted details to issue their decision, or such longer period as may be agreed in writing (see Article 24 of the GDO). Development undertaken in breach of the conditions imposed by the Order or by the local planning authority may be the subject of enforcement action.

C6   The Secretaries of State attach great importance to the prompt and efficient handling of applications for determination and of any subsequent submissions of details for approval under the provisions of the GDO. Undue delays can have serious consequences for agricultural and forestry businesses, which are more dependent than most on seasonal and market considerations. The procedures adopted by authorities should be straightforward, simple, and easily understood. Delegation of decisions to officers will help to achieve prompt and efficient handling, and should be extended as far as possible. Authorities should use their discretion over consulting parish/community councils and other groups about particular proposals, having regard to the need to reach decisions within the required timescales. Requests for more time from consultees should not be used as a reason for requiring the submission of details.

C7   Authorities should prepare forms which developers can use to apply for determination, along the lines of the example in the Appendix. This will help to minimise the number of cases in which submission of details may be necessary. Authorities should acknowledge the receipt of the written description, giving the date of receipt. Where the authority do not propose to require the submission of details, it would be helpful and courteous to inform the developer as soon as possible, to avoid any unnecessary delay or uncertainty.

C8 There will often be scope for informal negotiations with the developer, as an alternative or preliminary to requiring a formal submission of details. Developers for their part may find it useful to provide more than the minimum information required by the Order when informing authorities of their proposals, if this is readily available. For example, a sketch showing the proposed elevation of a building may clarify the effect of the proposal. If, as a result of discussions, the developer's original proposal is modified by agreement, he or she is not required to re-submit it formally to the authority in order to comply with the terms of the GDO condition, but the authority should give their written approval to the modification to make it clear that the developer has authority to proceed with the modified proposals.

C9 Planning authorities should generally be able to deal with applications on the basis of their experience and the information provided. Where authorities do not have the necessary expertise to consider the operational requirements of the agricultural or forestry enterprise, they may need to seek a technical appraisal. Where this is necessary they should aim to do this within the 28 day period, and not simply call for details on a precautionary basis. Extending the decision period may hamper business operations unreasonably.

Scope of controls

C10 The new arrangements do not impose full planning controls over the developments to which they apply – those developments remain "permitted development" under the GDO. The principle of development, and other planning issues, will not be relevant. When details are submitted for approval under the terms of the GDO, the objective should be to consider the effect of the development upon the landscape in terms of visual amenity, as well as the desirability of preserving ancient monuments and their settings, known archaeological sites, listed buildings and their settings, and sites of recognised nature conservation value (ie SSSIs and Local Nature Reserves). Details should be regarded in much the same light as applications for approval of reserved matters following the grant of outline planning permission. Subject to the normal criteria governing the use of conditions in planning permission, conditions may be imposed when approval is given. (DOE Circular 185 (Welsh Office 1/85) gives further advice in this respect.) Developers required to submit details for approval will have the right of appeal to the Secretary of State if approval is refused or is granted subject to conditions with which they disagree, or if notice of a decision on the details submitted is not given within the normal 8 week period. There is no right of appeal against the decision of a local planning authority to require approval of details. No compensation is payable under Section 108 of the Town and Country Planning Act 1990 if approval of submitted details is withheld by the planning authority.

C11 Special considerations apply to forestry roads. The intention to construct a new forest road is already often specified in Plans of Operations which come to the Forestry Commission as part of applications for approval for grant aid. Such applications are subject to the consultation procedures operated by the Commission with local authorities and other bodies. The procedures provide that if there is an objection from a local authority which cannot be resolved the Commission cannot approve such plans without reference to Ministers. The Commission intends to amend its rules so that in future Plans of Operations will include details of any new roads to be constructed. This will ensure that the environmental acceptability of new roads and the siting and landscaping of the woodland are considered together. The Secretaries of State would not expect local planning authorities to exercise their right to call for full details of roads which had been included in a Plan of Operations approved by the Forestry Commission after consultation with the authority. They would expect normally to allow appeals against refusal of permission for details in such circumstances.

Siting, design and appearance

C12 Local planning authorities may concern themselves with:

– the siting, design and external appearance of a proposed new agricultural or forestry building and its relationship to its surroundings;

– the siting and means of construction of roads;

– the siting of those excavations or waste deposits which individually or collectively exceed 0.5 hectare within the unit; and

– the siting and appearance of fish tanks (cages).

To ensure consistency of decision taking, and to help applicants, local planning authorities should consider preparing guidelines on the principles which they would wish to be taken into account when details of such buildings' design, materials and siting are being prepared. Such guidelines are an aid to communication, both with developers and with the agricultural buildings industry. The guidelines should identify where possible the situations or circumstances in which authorities would normally require the submission of details. They should preserve the scope for flexibility of approach; and note that the combination of siting, design and colour can particularly influence the degree of intrusion. Guidelines should not need to cover forest road construction, on which the Forestry Commission will be making its own guidance available.

C13 In preparing guidelines, authorities should consult those with an interest, for example local farming and conservation interests and the appropriate local office of MAFF or the Welsh Office. Continuing liaison with building designers and contractors will be important. Many farmers seek planning and design advice from building contractors and such advice ought to reflect the policies and practices of the local planning authority. Planning authorities' attention is drawn to British Standard BS5502 'Buildings and Structures for Agriculture', Part 20 'Code of Practice for general design considerations', which gives information on matters referred to in this guidance, together with reference to choice of colours and their use. Local planning authorities may find the following advice helpful in preparing guidelines.

Siting

C14   The siting of a new agricultural or forestry building, road, excavation or waste deposit, or fish tank can have a considerable impact on the site and the surrounding landscape. Developments should be assimilated into the landscape without compromising the functions they are intended to serve. New buildings should normally form part of a group rather than stand in isolation, and relate to existing buildings in size and colour. (New buildings of modern design may sometimes best be separated from a group of traditional buildings to avoid visual conflict.) Sites on skylines should be avoided if possible. To reduce their visual impact buildings should be blended into the landscape or, on sloping sites, set into the slope if that can be achieved without disproportionate cost.

C15   While a well sited building or road may benefit from some additional screening, the visual impact of a poorly situated one cannot easily be reduced. In some cases a minor repositioning or realignment can considerably improve the proposals. In others, a site elsewhere on the agricultural land would be preferable if this can be achieved without imposing undue operational or constructional difficulties. The options for siting of agricultural buildings and private ways will be influenced by their functional relationship to other buildings and services, so that alternatives may be limited. Where constructional problems emerge *after* proposals have been notified or approved, authorities will need to take a flexible approach to requests for approval of departures from the original proposals.

C16   The siting of new agricultural or forestry buildings adjacent (but not too close) to existing woods may help to assimilate them into the landscape. Suitable woodland management is required to maintain this effect. Elsewhere judicious tree planting and external works may enhance new buildings. The aim should not be to hide a building from sight, but rather to soften a hard outline, break up a prominent silhouette, and help 'anchor' a new building to the surrounding landscape. Any new planting should reflect the vegetation type already existing in the locality.

Design and appearance

C17   In exercising control over the design and external appearance of proposed developments, local planning authorities should have regard to the guidance contained in the Department of the Environment/Welsh Office Planning Policy Guidance Note 1. In general, while authorities should reject obviously poor designs, they should not interfere with the detailed design of buildings unless the sensitive character of the setting for the development justifies it.

C18   The choice of design and materials, and the relationships of texture and colour to existing development, local traditions, and the landscape, can be important considerations for both agricultural/forestry buildings and roads. For example, a single large building may have a greater impact on the countryside than one or more smaller buildings, which can be more easily incorporated into an existing group and provide greater flexibility. Roof overhang reduces apparent scale, as does the use of different materials for roof and walls. Well designed features such as rainwater downpipes and gutters, ventilators, eaves and gable overhang emphasise the shape of a building.

C19   The colours chosen should be compatible with the rural setting, not to camouflage the building, but to allow it to relate to existing buildings. Careful choice of colour reduces the apparent scale of a large agricultural building (eg if the roof of a building is coloured darker than the walls, its visual impact on its surroundings is reduced). The use of reflective materials should be avoided.

C20   Guidelines may include information on local building design. Traditional building styles may be important in devising local design criteria for modern buildings. It will normally be appropriate to use traditional or sympathetic materials for developments taking place in the setting of a listed building or in a conservation area.

C21   Alterations and extensions should not pose the same difficulty as new buildings, but similar considerations concerning design and appearance should be taken into account. Materials similar to the original should normally be used.

C22   Although choices of design and materials may be constrained by operational needs, the standardisation of modern agricultural buildings and economic considerations, it should be possible to reconcile proposals for development with the need to conserve and wherever possible enhance the landscape.

Crown development

C23   Development by the Forestry Commission is Crown development. In carrying out developments of the types described in this guidance, the Commission and other Crown developers will follow the procedure for notifying local planning authorities described in DOE Circular 18/84 (Welsh Office 37/84).

ANNEX D: RE-USE AND ADAPTATION OF RURAL BUILDINGS

D1 This guidance supplements that in paragraph 2.15, and should be read in conjunction with it.

D2 When assessing planning applications for the re-use or adaptation of a rural building, the primary consideration should be whether the nature and extent of the new use proposed for the building are acceptable in planning terms. It should not normally be necessary to consider whether the building is no longer needed for its present agricultural or other purposes (although, in the case of a tenanted agricultural building, the value in planning terms of the existing use should be taken into consideration). Evidence that a building is not redundant for its present use is not by itself sufficient grounds for refusing permission for a proposed new use. However, in circumstances where planning authorities have reasonable cause to believe that an applicant has attempted to abuse the system by constructing a new farm building with the benefit of permitted development rights, with the intention of early conversion to another use, it will be appropriate to investigate the history of the building to establish whether it was ever used for the purpose for which it was claimed to have been built.

D3 Where there are sound planning reasons for wishing to control the replacement of old farm buildings by new ones, a local planning authority may wish to consider attaching to the grant of planning permission for the use of agricultural buildings for non-agricultural purposes a condition withdrawing permitted development rights for new farm buildings in respect of that particular agricultural unit or holding. This course will generally only be appropriate where proliferation of farm buildings could have a seriously detrimental effect on the landscape. Such a condition should be used with great care, and must fairly and reasonably relate to the proposed development. While a restriction on additions to a particular group of farm buildings without specific permission might be reasonable, a restriction which sought to cover the whole of a large holding in connection with the re-use of a single building might well be unreasonable.

D4 If a planning application is submitted for the re-use of a building which the local planning authority considers has a significant adverse effect on the landscape in terms of visual amenity, it may be appropriate in connection with any proposed structural changes to impose conditions to secure an improvement in the external appearance of the building. Buildings which have become so derelict that they could be brought back into use only by complete or substantial reconstruction do not fall within the scope of the advice in the above paragraphs.

D5 Local planning authorities should examine applications for changes to residential use with particular care. The advice in paragraph D4 is often particularly relevant to such proposals. New housing in the open countryside is subject to strict control (see paragraph 2.18); it may be appropriate to apply similar principles to proposals for the conversion of existing rural buildings to dwellings, especially where such buildings are unsuitable for conversion without extensive alteration, rebuilding and/or extension. Residential conversions can often have detrimental effects on the fabric and character of historic farm buildings. While new uses can frequently be the key to the preservation of historic buildings, it is important to ensure that the new use is sympathetic to the rural character. In addition, the creation of a residential curtilage around a newly converted building can sometimes have a harmful effect on the character of the countryside, especially in areas of high quality landscape, including National Parks and Areas of Outstanding Natural Beauty.

D6 Residential conversions have a minimal impact on the rural economy. However conversions for holiday use can contribute more, and may reduce pressure to use other houses in the area for holiday use. Separate considerations apply to agricultural dwellings (see Annex E).

D7 If a building is listed, listed building consent will be needed for its conversion as well as planning permission.

ANNEX E: AGRICULTURAL AND FORESTRY DWELLINGS

E1 One of the few circumstances in which isolated residential development in the countryside may be justified is when accommodation is required to enable farm or forestry workers to live at or in the immediate vicinity of their place of work. Normally it will be as convenient for such workers to live in nearby towns or villages as it will be for them to live where they work. This may have domestic and social advantages as well as avoiding potentially intrusive development in the countryside.

E2 There will be some cases, however, in which the demands of the farming or forestry work concerned may make it essential for one or more of the people engaged in this work to live at or very close to the site of their work. Whether this is essential in any particular case will depend on the needs of the farm or forestry enterprise concerned and not on the personal preferences or circumstances of any of the individuals involved.

E3 Despite planning policies that impose strict controls on new residential development in the open countryside, the demand for such development remains high. Some of this demand may be justified by the genuine needs of farming and forestry, but some is speculative and stems from applicants seeking to exploit the physical or financial advantages of a new house in the countryside. It is, therefore, essential that all applications for planning permission for new agricultural or forestry dwellings are scrutinised thoroughly with the aim of detecting attempts to abuse the concession that the planning system makes for such dwellings.

E4 In particular, it will be important to establish that stated intentions to engage in farming or forestry are genuine, are reasonably likely to materialise and are capable of being sustained for a reasonable period of time. It will also be important to establish that the needs of the intended enterprise require one or more of the people engaged in it to live nearby. In assessing applications for new agricultural or forestry dwellings local planning authorities may therefore find it useful to apply functional and financial tests.

E5 A *functional test* will be necessary in all cases to establish whether it is essential for the proper functioning of the enterprise for one or more workers to be readily available at most times. Such a requirement might arise, for example, if workers are needed to be on hand day and night:

– in case animals or agricultural processes require essential care at short notice;

– to deal quickly with emergencies that could otherwise cause serious loss of crops or products, for example by frost damage or the failure of automatic systems.

E6 The protection of livestock from theft or injury by intruders may contribute on animal welfare grounds to the need for an agricultural dwelling, although it will not by itself be sufficient to justify one. Requirements arising from food processing, as opposed to agriculture, cannot be used to justify an agricultural dwelling. Nor can agricultural needs justify the provision of new dwellings as retirement homes for farmers.

E7 In determining whether a functional requirement exists it will be reasonable to consider not only the requirements of an enterprise as it exists at present but also its likely future requirements, provided there is clear evidence of a firm intention and ability to develop the farming or forestry business concerned.

E8 When a functional requirement is established, it will then be necessary to consider the number of workers needed to meet that requirement, for which the scale and nature of the enterprise will be relevant, and the extent to which any existing accommodation in the area is suitable and available for occupation by the workers concerned. When existing accommodation is insufficient, or where none exists, it may be appropriate for planning permission to be granted for one or more dwellings, provided other normal planning requirements, for example on siting and access, are also satisfied. Care should be taken to choose a site which is well related to existing farm buildings or other dwellings. Such dwellings should be of a size commensurate with the established functional requirement. Dwellings which are unusually large in relation to the agricultural needs of the unit, or unusually expensive to construct in relation to the income it can sustain in the long-term, should not normally be permitted. It is the requirements of the enterprise rather than of the owner or occupier which are relevant to determining whether or not a new dwelling is justified.

E9 In cases where a functional test alone is not conclusive, it may be appropriate also to apply a *financial test* to provide further evidence of the genuineness of stated intentions to engage in farming or forestry or the size of dwelling which the unit can sustain. The purpose of applying such a financial test is not to judge the likely present or future financial viability of the enterprise as such, since this is not a proper concern of the planning system, but to consider the land use implications for the site, which may include the likelihood of the proposed development being carried into effect and the size of dwelling. It therefore follows that an applicant should not be required to submit excessively detailed business accounts or projections in support of an application.

E10 Nevertheless it will be reasonable to assume that applicants who can demonstrate that an existing farm or forestry business is financially sound or that a proposed business has been planned on a sound financial basis are more genuine in their intentions than those unable to produce such evidence. Financial information about an existing or intended enterprise should therefore be regarded as complementary to other information submitted with an application for an agricultural or forestry dwelling.

E11   Whether it will be appropriate to apply a financial test as well as a functional one, and the rigour with which each test should be applied, will depend on the circumstances of each case. Financial evidence should normally be taken into account where the application for a dwelling relates to the intention to set up a completely new farm business. It may also be relevant where an application relates to an existing farm business and is associated with a major change in the nature or scale of the business. In both situations, significant investment in new farm buildings is often a good indication of intentions.

E12   The functional and financial tests may not need to be applied so rigorously to an application for an additional agricultural dwelling on an established farm, to meet an increased need for accommodation. On the other hand, in cases where the local planning authority is particularly concerned about possible abuse, it may be helpful to investigate the history of the holding to establish the recent pattern of use of land and buildings and whether, for example, any dwellings have recently been sold separately from the farmland concerned. Such a sale could constitute evidence of lack of agricultural need. Local planning authorities should, however, endeavour to minimise the information required of applicants, consistent with the level of scrutiny required in each case.

E13   In cases where there is evidence supporting an application for an agricultural or forestry dwelling but it is inconclusive, perhaps because there is uncertainty about the sustainability of a proposed enterprise, the local planning authority will wish to consider whether to grant permission for the provision of a caravan or other temporary accommodation on the site to allow time for such prospects to be clarified. If such permission is granted, the planning authority should make clear the period for which the permission is granted (two or three years should normally be sufficient) and the requirements that will have to be met when it expires if a permanent permission is then to be granted. It will normally be unsatisfactory to grant successive extensions to a temporary permission. In considering applications for temporary accommodation, authorities should normally work on the basis that it will be translated into a permanent dwelling if the agricultural unit proves viable. Thus they should not normally grant temporary permissions in locations where they would not permit a permanent dwelling.

E14   Local planning authorities are able where necessary to control the siting of agricultural buildings erected under permitted development rights. When they are considering the siting of such buildings, the possible need for an agricultural dwelling in connection with them is capable of being a material consideration.

E15   Where the need to provide accommodation to enable farm or forestry workers to live at or near their place of work has been accepted as justifying isolated residential development in the countryside, it will be necessary to ensure that the dwellings are kept available for meeting this need. For this purpose planning permission will normally be made subject to an occupancy condition. The following model condition is recommended:

> "The occupation of the dwelling shall be limited to a person solely or mainly working, or last working, in the locality in agriculture or in forestry, or a widow or widower of such a person, and to any resident dependents."

E16   It should not be necessary to tie occupation of the dwelling to workers engaged in one specific farm or forestry business even though the needs of that business justified the provision of the dwelling. The model occupancy condition recommended above will, however, ensure that the dwelling is kept available to meet the needs of other farm or forestry businesses in the locality if it is no longer needed by the original business, thus avoiding a proliferation of dwellings in the open countryside.

E17   When granting permission for a new agricultural dwelling, local planning authorities should be aware of the scope for imposing an occupancy condition not only on the dwelling itself but also on any existing dwellings on the unit which are under the control of the applicant, do not have occupancy conditions and need at the time of the application to be used in connection with the farm. This should help to protect the countryside against the risk of pressure for new houses. In appropriate circumstances, authorities may use planning obligations to tie a farmhouse to adjacent farm buildings, to prevent them being sold separately without further application to the authority. Advice on the use of planning obligations is given in DOE Circular 16/91 (Welsh Office 53/91). Where the application concerns a new enterprise, authorities may use conditions to prevent occupation of an agricultural dwelling until other works necessary for the establishment of the enterprise have been completed.

E18   Changes in the scale and character of farming and forestry in response to market changes may affect the longer term requirement for dwellings for which permission has been granted subject to an occupancy condition of the type set out above. Such dwellings should not be kept vacant, nor should their present occupants be unnecessarily obliged to remain in occupation simply by virtue of planning conditions restricting occupancy which have outlived their usefulness. Applications for the removal of occupancy conditions should be considered on the basis of realistic assessments of the continuing need for them, bearing in mind that it is the need for a dwelling for someone solely, mainly or last working in agriculture in an *area* as a whole and not just on the particular holding that is relevant.

E19 Planning authorities should be able to determine most applications for agricultural and forestry dwellings in the countryside, including cases involving the imposition or removal of occupancy conditions, on the basis of their experience and the information provided by the applicant and any other interested parties. If this is not the case, the Ministry of Agriculture, Fisheries and Food or the Welsh Office will be prepared to give a technical appraisal, which will be confined to a factual statement of the agricultural considerations involved and an evaluation of the specific points on which advice is sought; no recommendation for or against the application will be made. They will charge for such appraisals. Agricultural consultants may also be able to give advice.

ANNEX F: DEVELOPMENT INVOLVING HORSES

F1   High standards of design, construction and maintenance of buildings and care of land are necessary to ensure that equestrian activities do not have an adverse effect on the countryside and that the horses are well housed and cared for.

F2   As for all development in the countryside, applicants for planning permission for development involving horses should take particular care to minimise the effect their proposals will have on the appearance of the countryside. Buildings should be sited and designed to blend with their surroundings. Applicants may need to undertake to remove jumps and other equipment when not in frequent use; attention to design and maintenance may help reduce possible concerns about the unsightly nature of some jumps and equipment. Applicants may also be invited to assess the affects of their proposed development on erosion, and on the vegetation of the land to be used. When considering such planning applications, local planning authorities should bear in mind recommended standards for the safety and comfort of horses as well as other material planning considerations. Further advice, including a code of practice for horse owners and riders, is given in a booklet entitled "Horses in the Countryside" published by the Countryside Commission.

F3   Whether planning permission is needed for the use of land and buildings for horses and equestrian activities depends in some cases on whether the horses are used for agricultural, recreational or commercial purposes. The "use of land as grazing land" (which is part of the definition of agriculture in section 336 of the Town and Country Planning Act 1990) is widely taken to include the grazing of horses used for any purpose and so does not require planning permission; buildings used for housing horses used in farming qualify as agricultural development and so benefit from the permitted development rights in Part 6 of the GDO (see Annex B); and stables or loose-boxes erected within the curtilage of a dwellinghouse (ie in a large garden but not a separate paddock) for horses kept as "pet animals ... for the domestic needs or personal enjoyment of the occupants of the dwellinghouse" enjoy permitted development rights under Part 1 of the GDO.

F4   However, "the breeding and keeping of livestock" (also part of the definition of agriculture) has been held to relate only to livestock bred or kept for agricultural purposes. A full planning application is, therefore, normally required for the use of land for keeping horses for non-agricultural purposes and for buildings to house them unless these qualify as permitted development under Part 1 of the GDO.

THE TOWN AND COUNTRY PLANNING GENERAL DEVELOPMENT ORDER, SCHEDULE 2, PARTS 6 & 7

Model determination form

● **Notes for Guidance**

[NB Some provisions vary according to whether proposed development is on Article 1(6) land. Local planning authorities may wish to reflect their own situations]

1. Anyone proposing to carry out certain agricultural and forestry developments permitted under Parts 6 and 7 of the Town and Country Planning General Development Order (the GDO) must apply to the local planning authority in advance for a 'determination' as to whether the authority's prior approval of certain details of the development is required. This form is provided for that purpose. It is not suitable if a specific planning application is required – a separate planning application form is available from the local planning authority.

2. Part 6 of Schedule 2 to the GDO grants permitted development rights for a range of agricultural buildings and operations. Rights for erecting, extending or altering a building, and for excavations and engineering operations, are available to **larger agricultural units**, of at least 5 hectares. More limited rights, including extensions and alterations adding not more than 10% to the content of the original building, are available to **smaller units** of at least 0.4 hectares.

3. Rights for larger units are not available on separate parcels of land of less than 1 hectare, while rights for smaller units are not available on separate parcels of less than 0.4 hectare. Parcels may be separated from the rest of the unit by, for example, land in different ownership or a public road. The rights are subject to various other conditions.

4. Anyone proposing to carry out certain permitted development must inform the local planning authority in advance, so that it can if necessary control certain details. (The details concerned are the siting of the development, as well as design and external appearance in the case of buildings, means of construction in the case of private ways, and appearance in the case of fish tanks (cages)). This condition applies on larger agricultural units to:

the erection, extension or alteration of a building (but see note 6 below):

the formation or alteration of a private way;

the carrying out of certain excavations and waste deposits (see note 7 below);

the placing or assembly of a tank or cage for use in fish farming in any waters;

and on smaller agricultural units in National Parks and some adjoining areas ('Article 1(6) land') to:

the extension or alteration of a building; and

the provision, rearrangement or replacement of a private way.

5. Part 7 of Schedule 2 to the GDO grants permitted development rights for various forestry buildings and operations. A similar condition applies to:

the erection, extension or alteration of a building (but see paragraph 6 below): and

the formation or alteration of a private way.

6. On Article 1(6) land intending developers must inform the local planning authority of all proposed extensions and alterations to agricultural and forestry buildings under permitted development rights. Outside Article 1(6) land the requirement applies only to 'significant' extensions and alterations (ie where the cubic content of the original building would be exceeded by more than 10% or the height of the original building would be increased). Significant extensions and alterations may only be carried out once under permitted development rights.

7. The determination arrangements apply to proposed excavations and deposits of waste material which exceed 0.5 hectares in area, either individually or together with the aggregate of (a) the areas of all other unfilled excavations within the agricultural unit, and (b) all other parts of the unit on or under which waste has been deposited and has not been removed.

8. What constitutes an 'alteration' or 'rearrangement' for a farm or forestry road will be a matter of fact and degree depending on the circumstances of the case. If you intend to carry out works to an existing road, you should contact the local planning authority in advance to discuss the proposal.

9. The form needs to be accompanied by the appropriate fee of £20 (unless the proposed development is the carrying out of excavations, the deposit of waste or the placing or assembly of a tank or cage for use in fish farming, in which case no fee is payable).

....continued overleaf

● What you need to do

Please provide details of the development on the attached form. Complete sections 1 and 7 and whichever of sections 2, 3, 4, 5, and 6 are appropriate. The form must be accompanied by a site plan (not less than 1:1250) showing the location of the proposed building, road or excavation/waste deposit or fish tank (cage).

It will help if you discuss your proposal beforehand by contacting an officer of the authority.

Your contact is:

The completed form (along with your fee of £20 for development referred to in sections 2 and 3 of the form) should be returned to :

● What happens next

The authority has 28 days from receipt of this form to respond. You should receive an acknowledgement informing you of the date of receipt. If they later indicate that they are content (or do not respond within the 28 day period) then the development can proceed exactly as notified.

If informal discussions take place with the authority and the original proposal is modified by agreement, there is no requirement to re-submit to the authority. The authority should give written approval to the modification to make it clear that the modified proposals can proceed.

If the authority indicate, within the 28 day period, that they require the formal submission of details for approval, work cannot begin until details have been approved by the authority. Their decision should normally be issued within 8 weeks of receiving the details.

If approval is refused, or is granted subject to conditions with which you disagree, you have the right to appeal – within six months – to the Secretary of State (for the Environment) (for Wales).

THE TOWN AND COUNTRY PLANNING GENERAL DEVELOPMENT
ORDER, SCHEDULE 2, PARTS 6 & 7

Model determination form

● Please detach and read the Notes for Guidance before completing this form.

● **Do not** start work until :
  - the authority have notified you in writing that prior approval is not required; **or**
  - you have received approval from the authority; **or**
  - at least 28 days have elapsed from the date your form was **received** by the authority, and they have not notified you that prior approval is or is not required.

● If completing this form by typewriter, please use the alignment guidelines in the margins of each page.

1. The site

i. Name and address of person(s) submitting this form

Telephone

ii. Name and address of farm and occupier (if different from i. above)

Telephone

iii. What is the area of the agricultural unit?
Agricultural unit means agricultural land which is occupied as a unit for the purposes of agriculture

hectares

iv. What is the area of the parcel of land where the development is to be located? (see note 3)

| *1 hectare or more* | *less than 1 hectare but at least 0.4 hectare* | *less than 0.4 hectare* |

v. What is the Ordnance Survey grid reference of the proposed development?

vi. Does the proposed development affect an ancient monument, archaeological site, listed building; or is it within a site of special scientific interest or a local nature reserve?

Y or N

If *Yes*, please provide details

FED 0422 (12/91) OSD2   3

2. The proposed building (please enclose a site plan and indicate whether a new building, extension or alteration is involved)

i.   Type of building

ii. Dimensions

length [ ] *metres*

breadth [ ] *metres*

height to eaves [ ] *metres*

height to ridge [ ] *metres*

iii. Walls

materials [ ]

external colour [ ]

iv. Roof

materials [ ]

external colour [ ]

v.   Has an agricultural building been constructed on this unit within the last two years? [ ] *Y or N*

If *Yes,*

what is its overall ground area? [ ] *square metres*

what is its distance from the proposed new building? [ ] *metres*

3. The proposed road (please enclose a site plan and indicate if a new road or alteration is involved)

i.   Dimensions

length [ ] *metres*

width [ ] *metres*

ii. Surface materials

materials [ ]

colour [ ]

4

4. The proposed excavation/deposit of waste material from the farm (please enclose a site plan)

i. What is the area of the proposed works? [   ] *hectares*

ii. Please provide details of the works

[   ]

iii. Have previous excavations or waste deposits been carried out? (see note 7)   [   ] *Y or N*

If *Yes*, please give the area of the previous works   [   ] *hectares*

5. The proposed fish tank (cage) (please enclose a site plan)

i. Please provide details, including dimensions, materials and appearance

[   ]

6. Fee

i. Please confirm you have included your fee of £20 (for development in section 2 or 3) by ticking this box   [   ]

7. Signature

Signature

[   ]

Name (BLOCK CAPITALS)

[   ]

Date

[   ]

5

Printed in the United Kingdom for HMSO
Dd.295801, 3/92, C50, 3390/3, 5673, 191048

HMSO publications are available from:

HMSO Publications Centre
(Mail, fax and telephone orders only)
PO Box 276, London, SW8 5DT
Telephone orders 071-873 9090
General enquiries 071-873 0011
(queuing system in operation for both numbers)
Fax orders 071-873 8200

HMSO Bookshops
49 High Holborn, London, WC1V 6HB   071-873 0011 (counter service only)
258 Broad Street, Birmingham, B1 2HE   021-643 3740
Southey House, 33 Wine Street, Bristol, BS1 2BQ   (0272) 264306
9-21 Princess Street, Manchester, M60 8AS   061-834 7201
80 Chichester Street, Belfast, BT1 4JY   (0232) 238451
71 Lothian Road, Edinburgh, EH3 9AZ   031-228 4181

HMSO's Accredited Agents
(see Yellow Pages)

and through good booksellers

£5.20 net

ISBN 0-11-752585-

9 780117 525856